YOU ME, AND
Anxiety

Take Action Over Anxiety to Enjoy Being You
JOURNAL

Dr. Robyn Reu Graham

ISBN: 978-1-956442-02-1

Published by Highlander Press
501 W. University Pkwy, Ste. B2
Baltimore, MD 21210

Cover design: Christy Collins of Constellation Book Services
Front cover image: imnoom, www.istockphoto.com
Interior Design: Patricia Creedon of Pat Creedon Design, Inc.
Editor: Deborah Kevin, MA
Author's photo credit: Aliza Schlabach

Printed in the United States of America

Action
Anxiety

Hey Beautiful!

Living with anxiety can feel overwhelming, exhausting, and hopeless. But it doesn't have to. I've created this tool for you to use to take action and navigate your anxiety, to feel hope and joy as you move through your journey of life.

This is the tool I wish I had had when I was young. It is my gift to you, to help you realize how truly amazing you are. To accept and embrace yourself exactly as you are.

I'm proud of you for taking action! It will make a difference.

With love and smiles,

Robyn

"You, Me, and Anxiety: Take Action Over Anxiety to Enjoy Being You" Journal

This workbook/journal is meant to accompany the book, "You, Me, and Anxiety: Take Action Over Anxiety to Enjoy Being You". This journal will become your haven for writing your thoughts, feelings, and taking action over your anxiety.

Each sample table in the book is represented here for you to journal your responses to the questions and suggested activities. Note that there are enough spaces for you to come back and reflect and journal time and time again. In addition, replacement journals are available if this becomes a long-term practice, which I highly recommend.

Prompts

Take time to look back at your life and notice how you felt and the decisions you made about experiences, circumstances, and relationships. Are there times in which you:

- Regret the decision you made;
- Missed out on something fun;
- Pulled away from a friend;
- Didn't feel good enough to participate in something;
- Felt like you didn't fit in;
- Had a fight with someone;
- Freaked out for no apparent reason;
- Felt super angry but didn't know why;
- Were too afraid to do something that you knew would be fun; or
- Didn't do something because you were afraid something bad would happen?

List the experiences, decisions, and how each made you feel physically.

What Was the Experience?	How Did I Physically Feel?
Trying out for the basketball team	Sick to my stomach
Asked to do a solo at the band concert	Headache, shaky, stomach pains
Packing for vacation	Tired, unable to focus
Didn't go to a party with a friend	Cried, exhausted, shaky, threw up

Do you see a pattern? Were there similar circumstances that you felt the same way about? Were there certain people involved with various experiences? Did you have the same physical symptoms around multiple scenarios that prevented you from having experiences? Was it a feeling of fear that held you back from each experience? Did you repeatedly react inappropriately to situations? If you had similar reactions, physically or emotionally, to a number of situations you can start to break down how anxiety is causing you to react and influencing the decisions you make.

Prompts

If you don't have someone to talk about your feelings of shame with, do the following exercise. This exercise is not meant to substitute human conversation but provide a temporary solution.

List your feelings of shame and then think of something positive and a reason that you can let go of that shame. As you go through this exercise, remember that shame is based on the fear that you are unlovable for whatever reason you've convinced yourself of.

The Feeling of Shame that is Consuming Me	Why I am Worthy and Can Release this Feeling of Shame
I was rude to my mom	*I apologized and mom forgave me*
I failed my geometry test, everyone else has a better grade	*I worked hard, I talked to my teacher, I have As in all of my other subjects*
I didn't make the basketball team	*I did my best, I can work hard and try again next year if I still want to make the team, I tried out even though I was afraid*

Prompts

Fear is a mechanism our brains were created with to protect us. It is not wrong to be afraid, but sometimes fears get in the way and prevent us from doing things and enjoying life. I want you to embrace fears you've had, but leave them here, right here on this page and move through each topic with an open mind and the goal of learning and growing to overcome the fear that has previously held you back.

Fearful Thought	Feelings created by the fearful thought	New positive thought	Feelings created by the new positive thought
No one likes me	Sad, lonely, afraid	Sara is my friend, and she is nice to me	Happy, content, excited
I am going to fail this geometry test	Sad, scared, overwhelmed, frustrated	I have been studying so much, and I met with my tutor, I will do my best	Relieved, nervous but confident
What if the plane crashes	Scared, overwhelmed, confused, conflicted, sad	I can't wait to see Grandma, plane crashes don't happen very often, my parents will be with me	Relieved, excited, happy

In the table below, list your fears. Then, from the list of Bible verses in the book, choose one that you can recite when you feel each fear encroaching on your sense of security and courage.

Fear	Bible Verse to Give You Courage
Doing a presentation	*"I can do all things through Him who gives me strength." Philippians 4:13.*

Prompts

Look at relationships with family and friends as necessities, we all need someone to love and someone to love us, but not at the expense of falling away from your values, morals, integrity, or losing your sense of self. Make a list your non-negotiables when it comes to relationships. These non-negotiables will help you make good decisions when it comes to choosing friends and taking action within relationships. We can't choose our family, but we can choose how we treat others and what we tolerate from others. Here are some of my non-negotiables that help me stay grounded in my relationships with friends and family members:

- Upholding my values
- Having integrity
- Being kind
- Being honest
- Living with empathy
- Being compassionate
- Walking in my faith
- Surrounding myself with positive people
- Protecting my body
- Staying healthy
- Getting enough sleep
- Journaling
- Daily devotions
- Prioritizing family
- Trust
- Integrity
- Forgiving myself and others for mistakes
- Focusing on daily gratitude

WHAT ARE YOUR NON-NEGOTIABLES?

My Non-Negotiables	Why This is Non-Negotiable
Honesty	I want people to trust me
Faith	It gives me hope, comfort, and peace
Being thoughtful	I want others to know I care about them
Getting enough sleep	I don't want to be crabby because I'm tired

Sometimes experiences stimulate anxiety, which appears in the form of physical symptoms. Let's call these things triggers. They are triggering an emotion or feeling that you don't like or aren't comfortable with. Track them and if you can identify where they begin, you can start avoiding them, challenging them, or changing them. This will help you spend more time in a neutral or happy place of feeling instead of feeling sad, anxious, angry, or frustrated or even from lashing out at others.

Doing this exercise will help you identify the emotions earlier in the process and help you navigate that emotion going forward.

What I'm Feeling	When Did the Feeling Start	What Was the Trigger
My stomach hurts	This morning	Geometry test
Tired	I couldn't sleep last night	Presentation

Once you have written about the feelings and triggers, journal around them. Writing can be very therapeutic and help you create a strategy for avoiding triggers in the future or react to or handle them more pleasantly.

Another key component of relationships is trust. If you really think about the people around you, who can you trust?

Make a list of them and note why you believe you can trust them and document any hesitation you feel come up when you write about them. If you have any hesitation, do not share your soul!

Who Do I Trust?	Why Do I Trust Them?	What Hesitation Do I Have About Trusting Them?
Mom	She has never let me down	Sometimes she doesn't understand me and gets angry when I can't do something because of my anxiety
Megan	She seems like a great friend	She's also friends with so and so and I am not comfortable around her, what if she tells so and so about me

Prompts

There are many lists of values available online and in books. A few values that are very important to me include faith, integrity, curiosity, gratitude, and service. Values are very specific to individuals. When you review a list of values you may find 15 or 20 that you immediately feel connected to. Once you have that list, review it, and decide if any of them are similar. If yes, decide which one you most connect with, and choose it. Do this exercise to narrow your core values down to 3 to 5 that you will not waiver on. Here's an example:

Top 10-15	Top 7-10	Top 3-5	Why?
Faith	Kindness	Faith	Because I know Jesus helps me every day
Hope	Creativity	Kindness	I want others to know I care about them and want to make them feel valued
Gratitude	Beauty	Creativity	I love to create, it gives me peace, and joy, and opportunity to change the world
Service	Friendships	Leadership	I want to lead by example and help others find their way to a great life
Compassion	Influence	Friendships	I want to be a true friend that others can depend on and trust

Curiosity	Leadership		
Beauty	Faith		
Adventure			
Creativity			
Kindness			
Leadership			
Authority			
Friendships			
Respect			
Religion			
Influence			

Now you try:

Top 10-15	Top 7-10	Top 3-5	Why?

Prompts

Remember when I said that it is best to treat yourself the way you treat others? You can also look at this as you get to treat yourself the way you want others to treat you. With that said, get out your journal and map out your thoughts around the invitation that is sitting on your desk. Decide, based on your thoughts and feelings what you want to do, what you think is best for you, and what will make you feel happy, content, and most comfortable. You may ultimately decide you want to go, or you may decide it is best for you not to go. But take time to decide, don't rush your decision. You can use this model (CTFAR) to unpack possibilities related to your decision:

- Circumstance
- Thoughts
- Feelings
- Action
- Results

Circumstance	Invitation to a party negative thoughts	Invitation to a party positive thoughts
Thoughts	I can't go. They might think I'm weird. I don't have cool clothes to wear. I just got my hair cut and it looks terrible. No one will talk to me.	I can do this. I want to make new friends. Jane invited me so I know she likes me and wants me to be there. Natalie will be there, too. I can wear the dress I wore for Sam's party last year. I'll curl my hair.
Feelings	FOMO. Sad, lonely, miserable, uncomfortable, angry, and ashamed.	Nervous but excited, happy, and confident.
Action	Sitting at home by yourself.	Go to the party.
Results	Go to bed sad and lonely. Mom and Dad asking what's wrong all night. Not invited to the next party.	Have fun. Make a new friend. Received a compliment on your dress. Invited to another party.

Here's a blank for you to use as a sample. If you like this prompt, feel free to copy it into another journal and use this technique as often as you like.

	Negative thoughts	Positive thoughts
Circumstance		
Thoughts		
Feelings		
Action		
Results		

Prompts

Having gratitude can help change your perspective on your life and relationships. Start now. List at least three things you are grateful for at this moment in time.

It is helpful to list at least three things that you are grateful for every night before you go to sleep. You'll close out your day recognizing good experiences versus allowing anxious thoughts or worries to creep in as you try to sleep.

Today I am Grateful For:	I am Grateful Because:
My mom	She always supports me.
My journal	I love having a safe place to share my thoughts and feelings.
My dog	Who doesn't need unconditional love?

The first C of the 5C's journaling method for navigating anxiety is catching the anxious or negative thoughts. When you experience anxiety or worry, recognize the thought that is triggering it.

In the book I shared an example of my anxiety around writing this book. Now it's your turn.

Here's a recap of the 5Cs journaling method in case you need them:

- **Catch** the anxious or negative thoughts and write them down.
- **Challenge** the anxious or negative thoughts. Are they realistic? What is the likelihood they will come to fruition? Can they be proven?
- **Change** the anxious or negative thoughts to positive thoughts. The positive thought is probably more likely to be a reality. Notice how you start to feel better once you have changed your thoughts.
- **Control** the thoughts. Journal around the positive thoughts and take action to make them come to reality. Create an affirmation around the positive thoughts.
- **Confidence** will grow as you recite the affirmation and focus on the positive thoughts. As confidence grows, your anxiety will decrease and you will make better decisions, take more action, and choose better behaviors.

Negative Thoughts	Rephrased Thoughts
No one will buy the book. I am not an expert at in anxiety. People will judge me if I publish this book.	If I write this book, people will buy it, this book will help others. There will be sales of this book if I write it.
What if people don't like this book?	People who have anxiety and need the book will love the book.
I am not an expert this book won't help anyone.	I have lived with anxiety my entire life and can help people if I share my experiences, thoughts, and feelings in this book.
I don't know how to publish a book.	Hire a publisher.
I'm not a good writer, there might be mistakes.	No one is perfect and it's the message that matters
What if I don't help anyone?	What if I help someone because she read the book and decided not to do drugs or die by suicide?

Prompts

Sometimes we need a little treat. But other times, we succumb to emotional eating that isn't a healthy practice. When you experience the later, write it down and keep track so that you can learn the foods and products that you need to avoid in the future. You can start here, and in the future use your journal as a log.

What I Ate	How I Felt
Ice Cream	Happy but then sad and mad
A salad	Healthy, content, satisfied
M & M candies	Happy because I shared them with Mom

Action

Anxiety

TAKE CONTROL OF YOUR ANXIETY
FOLLOW HEALTHY DAILY ROUTINE

When you make healthy decisions, you can reduce symptoms of anxiety.

HEALTHY HABITS FOR A HEALTHY MIND

☐ Make Your Bed

☐ Brush Your Teeth

☐ Wash Your Face

☐ Get Dressed

☐ Devotion/Meditation/Affirmation/Journal

☐ Eat a Healthy Breakfast

☐ School/Lunch/Practice/Activities

☐ Eat a healthy Dinner with Family

☐ Finish School Work or Studying

☐ Shower and Brush Teeth

☐ Journal & Practice Gratitude

☐ Get to Bed for 8 Hours of Sleep

The remainder of the journal is for you to use daily as a means of taking action over anxiety. Write your thoughts, affirmations, mantras, gratitude, feelings, emotions, and dreams. This is your place to navigate all things anxiety, fear, self-doubt, and worry and get them out of your head and onto paper.

DATE_____/_____/_____

DATE____/____/____

DATE____/____/____

DATE____/____/____

DATE_____/_____/_____

DATE____/____/____

DATE____/____/____

DATE ____ / ____ / ____

DATE_____/_____/_____

DATE _____ / _____ / _____

DATE_____ / _____ / _____

DATE_____ / _____ / _____

DATE_____ / _____ / _____

DATE_____ / _____ / _____

DATE____/____/____

DATE_____ / _____ / _____

DATE____/____/____

DATE ____ / ____ / ____

DATE_____/_____/_____

DATE ____ / ____ / ____

DATE ____ / ____ / ____

DATE ____ / ____ / ____

DATE____/____/____

DATE____ / ____ / ____

DATE ___ / ___ / ___

DATE_____/_____/_____

DATE_____ /_____ /_____

DATE____/____/____

DATE____/____/____

DATE_____ / _____ / _____

DATE____/____/____

DATE_____ /_____ /_____

DATE____/____/____

DATE ____ / ____ / ____

DATE_____/_____/_____

DATE____/____/____

DATE_____/_____/_____

DATE ____ / ____ / ____

DATE____/____/____

DATE_____/_____/_____

DATE____ /____ /____

DATE____/____/____

DATE____ / ____ / ____

DATE____/____/____

DATE ___/___/___

DATE____/____/____

DATE____ / ____ / ____

DATE____ / ____ / ____

DATE ____ / ____ / ____

DATE ____ / ____ / ____

DATE____/____/____

DATE ____ / ____ / ____

DATE ___ / ___ / ___

DATE____ / ____ / ____

DATE____ / ____ / ____

DATE____ / ____ / ____

DATE____/____/____

DATE ____ / ____ / ____

DATE ____ / ____ / ____

Dr. Robyn Graham is an anxious introvert on a mission to help teen girls go from feeling anxious to relentless by sharing her life-long journey with anxiety and the tools and resources that helped her not only survive but thrive. As a clinical pharmacist, professional photographer, brand strategist, and business coach, Robyn has witnessed both the clinical and social complications of anxiety and how it holds people, especially girls and women, back from achieving their goals and dreams. Robyn is a mom to Joshua, Samuel, and Grace, wife to Dr. John Graham, dog mom to Stella, and a daughter, sister, aunt, and friend. You, Me, and Anxiety is her first book.

You can follow Dr. Graham on the following social media channels:

- Facebook: https://www.facebook.com/therobyngraham
- Instagram: https://www.instagram.com/therobyngraham
- Twitter: https://twitter.com/therobyngraham
- LinkedIn: https://www.linkedin.com/in/therobyngraham

ABOUT THE PUBLISHER

 Highlander Press, founded in 2019, is a mid-sized publishing company committed to diversity and sharing big ideas thereby changing the world through words.

What makes Highlander Press unique is that their business model focuses on building strong collaborative relationships with other women-owned businesses, which specialize in some aspect of the publishing industry, such as graphic design, book marketing, book launching, copyrights, and publicity. The mantra "a rising tide lifts all boats" is one they embrace.

 facebook.com/highlanderpress

 instagram.com/highlanderpress

 linkedin.com/in/highlanderpress

CPSIA information can be obtained
at www.ICGtesting.com
Printed in the USA
BVHW050236190123
656577BV00007B/153